Contents

Australia and Asia

A child's life is like a piece of paper on which every person leaves a mark.

Chinese proverb

Asia is the largest continent in the world, both in its size and population. It covers an area of more than 44 million square kilometres (km^2) and has a growing population of more than 4 billion people. When you think of Asia, countries such as China, Indonesia and Thailand might spring to mind. However, there are more than 45 different countries that make up Asia, including Bhutan and Turkmenistan.

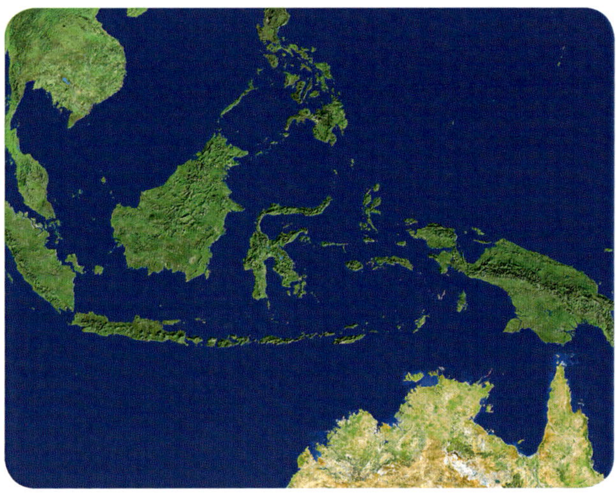

A satellite image of the continent of Asia and the top of Australia

Nearby is the smallest continent in the world – Australia. Its neighbouring countries include New Zealand, New Caledonia, Vanuatu, the Solomon Islands, Papua New Guinea and islands in South-East Asia, including Indonesia. Being a multicultural nation, Australia has become home to many people from all over the world. It is therefore important for Australians to understand, value and respect the diverse cultures of its citizens.

It is also important for Australians to develop and maintain a good relationship with other nations, especially its Asian neighbours, as many of these, including China and India, are fast-growing world **economies**. There is much to be gained from developing connections between Australia and Asia.

Did you know?
The Koreans and Vietnamese measure their age according to the number of **lunar** years they have lived through. Vietnamese New Year, or Tet, is considered to be everyone's birthday.

economies related to making and managing money
lunar to do with the moon

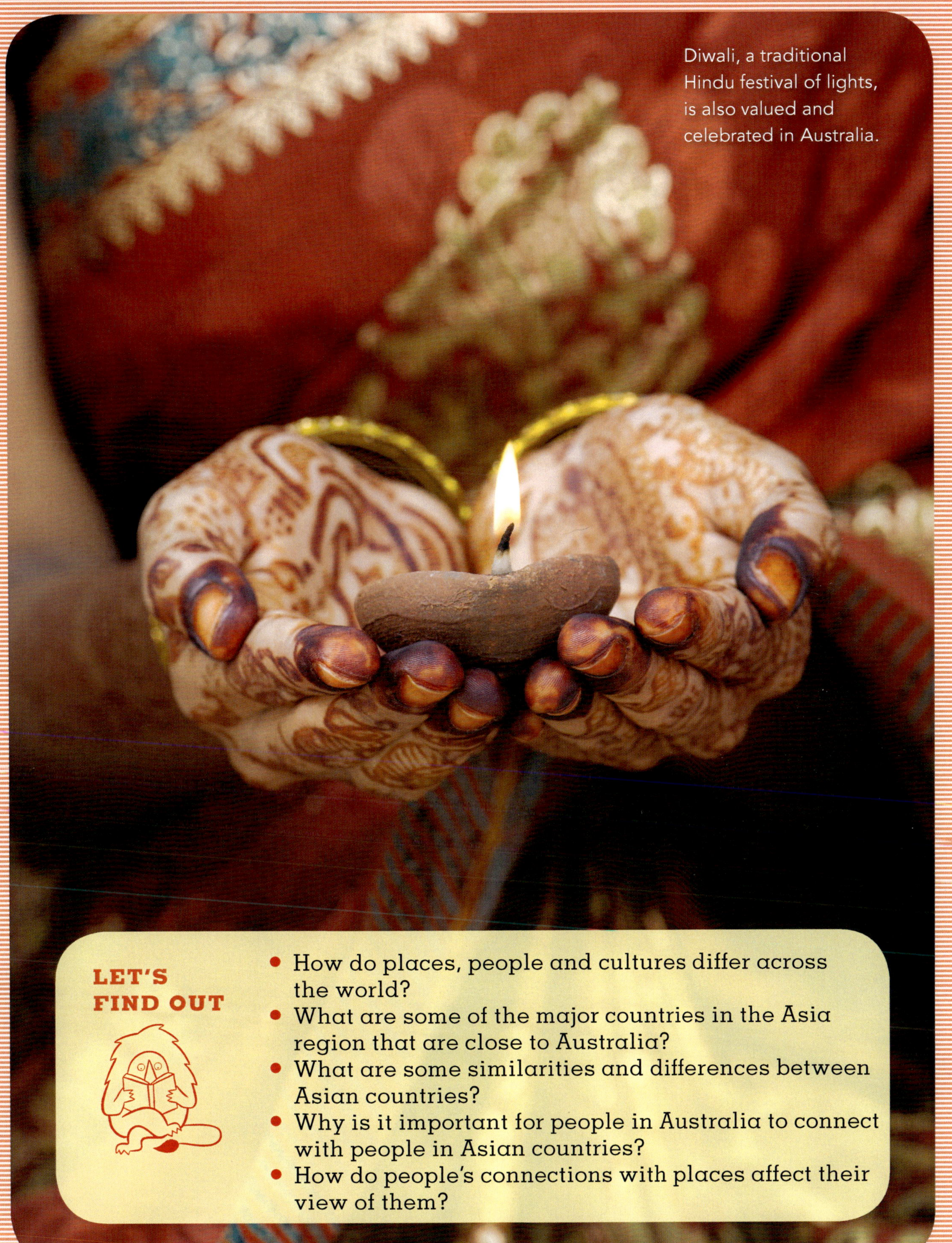

Diwali, a traditional Hindu festival of lights, is also valued and celebrated in Australia.

LET'S FIND OUT

- How do places, people and cultures differ across the world?
- What are some of the major countries in the Asia region that are close to Australia?
- What are some similarities and differences between Asian countries?
- Why is it important for people in Australia to connect with people in Asian countries?
- How do people's connections with places affect their view of them?

China

China is one of the largest and most populated countries on the planet. It is home to many different ethnic groups, who inhabit a country of extremes. In the west of China there are deserts and mountains, while in eastern China there are hills, plains and **river deltas**.

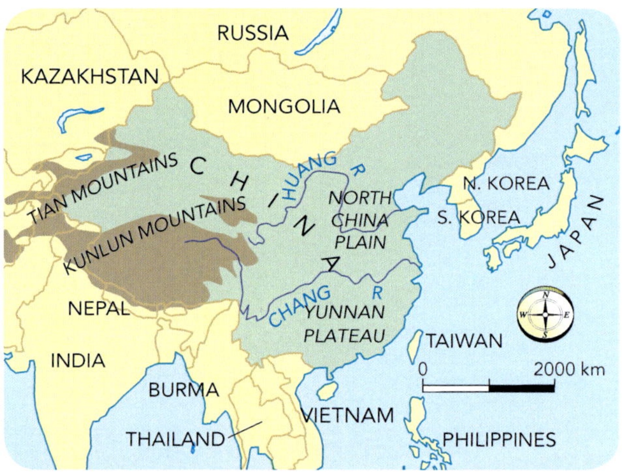

Fact File	
Population	1 349 585 838
Land area	9 596 961 km^2
Capital	Beijing
Largest city	Guangzhou
Main languages	Mandarin and Cantonese

Culture

China is considered by historians to have the longest continuous civilisation in the world, stretching back more than 4000 years. The Han dynasty began more than 2000 years ago and created an empire that valued art, technology and philosophy. More than 90 per cent of China's population consider themselves to be Han Chinese.

The Arts

The Chinese are well known for their great contribution to the Arts. Unique and beautiful paintings, sculptures, opera and dance have always been part of the Chinese culture. Some of their oldest treasures were made from clay, and include elaborate tiles, pots and figures.

Beautiful porcelain objects were often created for use in imperial courts. They were also given as gifts to other countries to demonstrate the wealth and power of the Chinese emperors.

In the 14th century, the cloisonné technique became widespread in China. This involved creating designs on metal objects using copper or bronze wires and coloured glass pastes. The item had to be fired in a kiln and polished before it was complete and ready for show.

A cloisonné vase being made by hand

river deltas the area at the end of rivers, near seas, lakes or oceans

Calligraphy is another traditional Chinese art form. Still very much practised today, calligraphers use a traditional method to write Chinese characters and paint images from nature on paper or silk using coloured inks and brushes.

The skills of jade sculptors are highly valued in China. They spend many years learning how to carve sculptures, bowls and jewellery. Jade is a valuable green Chinese stone and symbolises beauty, grace and purity.

Chinese acrobats have an international reputation for their precision and ablity to perform daring feats. The art of acrobatics has existed for more than 2000 years. Some traditional acts include the Lion Dance, wire walking, cycling feats and hoop diving.

Chinese acrobats performing a cycle feat

Inventions

The Chinese are well known for their inventions. They invented the first compass, clock, gunpowder and fireworks. They also introduced a number of paper products to the world, including paper money and toilet paper.

Traditions

The tea ceremony is an important ritual in Chinese life with many rules about how to serve and drink tea. Tea drinking became very popular during the Tang dynasty.

Traditional Chinese tea ceremony

Food

Often Chinese cities are known for a particular food speciality. The city of Beijing is known for its roast duck, while the city of Shanghai is famous for its dumplings. Northern food tends to feature oil, vinegar and garlic. Southern food consists of more rice and chilli peppers.

Leisure

Health and fitness are very important to the Chinese people. It is common to find hundreds of people engaged in a variety of sporting and leisure activities in local parks.

During the day many older Chinese people will gather in parks to sing, perform Tai Chi, play chess or fly kites. People of all age groups enjoy playing *jianzi*, or shuttlecock kicking, where the aim of the game is to kick a shuttlecock (made of feathers) from one person to another, without it touching the ground.

Young people in China also like to spend their leisure time shopping, playing with new digital technologies and engaging in popular culture.

Transport

There are many ways to travel in China, apart from by car, bus or airplane. In Shanghai you can travel to the airport on a Maglev train, which levitates on the track and travels at 300 km per hour. In the back streets of Shanghai you can ride in a **rickshaw** or brave the busy streets in a **tuk tuk**.

Interesting fact

Cars can only be driven on certain days in Beijing. The day depends on the final number on the car's numberplate. The number of cars on the road needs to be limited due to the huge population.

A Maglev train

Celebrations

Celebrating festivals with family is a very important part of the Chinese culture. Three important festivals are Chinese New Year, the Mid-Autumn (or Moon) festival and the Ghost festival. More people travel during the Chinese New Year than at any other time of the year. It is a time to visit family members and watch firework displays. During the Mid-Autumn festival, people eat moon cakes. During the Ghost festival, people burn fake paper money to make offerings to their ancestors.

Conclusion

China is a country with a rich history and culture. Its landscape and climate are as varied as its foods, traditions and achievements. It is a country that continues to grow in wealth and power.

rickshaw a small hand-pulled cart for one or two passengers
tuk tuk a motorised three-wheeled vehicle that carries one or two passengers

Breakaway tasks

Remembering

1 What is the capital of China?

2 Name two traditional Chinese art forms.

Understanding

3 Describe how to play the Chinese game of jianzi.

4 Use a Venn diagram to compare an important Chinese tradition with an Australian tradition.

Applying

5 Learn how to write your name using Chinese characters. Use a brush and ink to write your name on paper or silk.

Analysing

6 Devise a survey to find out how classmates spend their leisure time. Compare your findings to the information presented in the report. What are the similarities and differences?

7 Analyse the information and sub-titles in the report. Which areas would you change, add or remove if you were to write a report about a country?

Evaluating

8 Consider the difference between travelling in a rickshaw and a Maglev train. Use a PMI to evaluate the positive, negative and interesting aspects of using one of these forms of transport.

9 Discuss with a partner whether you would like to visit China, based on the information in the report. Write a letter to a parent, friend or teacher explaining why China would be a good holiday destination.

Creating

10 Research some traditional Chinese artworks, including those that use symbols or calligraphy and Chinese characters. Create your own art piece applying similar features to your work.

How to draw Manga

Manga is a style of Japanese comic that originated in the early 20th century. When Manga comics were first created they were not very popular. However, American comics such as *Captain America* and *Superman* had a significant influence on Manga artists and led them to create a more modern Manga style. Manga is now very popular throughout Asia and the world. Animated Manga is known as Anime. The Japanese pronunciation for Manga is 'maw-nnn-gah'.

Manga style is quite distinctive. Most characters have large eyes and big hair.

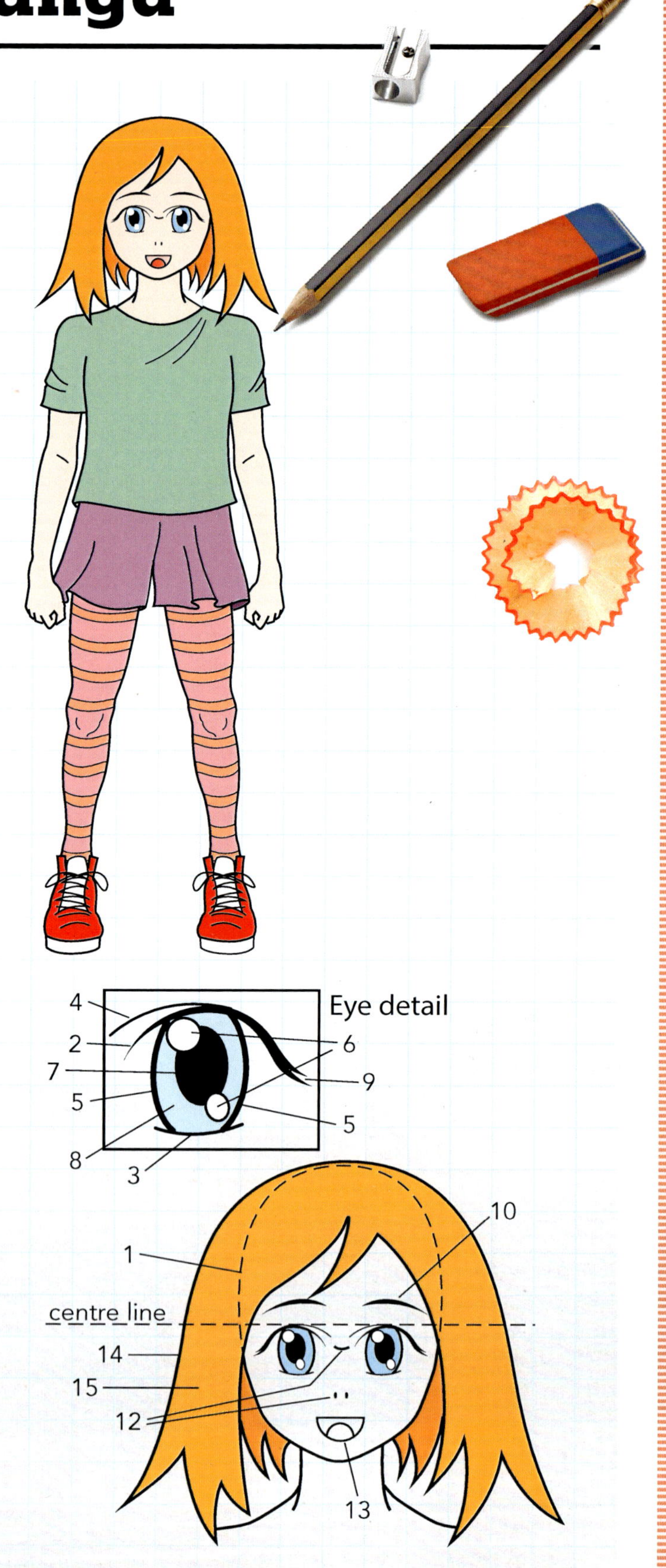

Materials

- Paper
- Grey-lead pencil
- Coloured pencils
- Black fine-tip pen

What to do

1 Draw an egg-shaped oval for the face, with a pointed chin.

2 In the centre of the face, create a thick curve for the first upper eyelid.

3 Draw a shorter, straighter line below for the lower part of the eye.

4 Draw a curved line above the upper eyelid.

5 Draw a wide oval for the iris.

6 Draw circles to show glare from the light source.

7 Draw a smaller oval in the middle of the iris for the pupil. Colour this black.

8 Shade or colour in the remainder of the iris, apart from the glare ovals.

9 Add eyelashes to the end of the eyelid.

10 Draw thin eyebrows.

11 Repeat steps 2 to 10 to draw the second eye.

12 Draw a fine line for the bridge of the nose, then add nostrils.

13 Add a small semicircle for the mouth. Another semicircle can be added for the tongue.

14 Draw a basic hair shape on your Manga. Add some thick and thin hair strands to show movement.

15 Colour in the hair with a bright colour, adding shading along the lines.

16 Draw the body.

17 Outline your Manga character using a black fine-tip pen and then use coloured pencils to complete your drawing.

Manga faces

Different facial expressions will require slight changes to the eyes, mouth and facial features. These features differ for female and male Manga characters.

Breakaway tasks

Remembering

1 What is Manga?

2 When was the first Manga created?

Understanding

3 Explain how Manga became popular.

4 Use a Similar and different graphic organiser to compare Manga and Anime.

Applying

5 Follow the instructions to create a new Manga character. Draw your new character with three different facial expressions.

Analysing

6 Look at the Manga characters in the procedure. Identify the key features of Manga characters and present your findings on a concept map.

7 Research some websites that show how to draw Manga. Explain the differences between drawing male and female Manga characters. Use a T-chart to record your findings.

Evaluating

8 In your opinion, what further steps could be added to the procedure for drawing Manga?

9 Carry out a class survey to identify students' favourite reading material. Present your findings on a graph. What percentage of students like reading cartoons best? Are there any generalisations you can draw from your data?

Creating

10 Design a new Manga character. Create a character profile, including an illustration, and information such as name, age hobbies and powers. Write a short paragraph about your character's physical appearance and personality.

My Asian adventure

Kate has set off on an adventure with her family. Read the email trail to find out more about her holiday.

Date: 10 September

Hi Jamie

We've just arrived in Timor Leste. It is very different from Australia. The weather is hot and humid. Houses in the countryside are simple, and most of the people work as farmers or weavers. The people are friendly and are keen to sell us their colourful, woven cloth, called *tais*. Did you know that books have only been written in Tetum (the language most commonly used by people in Timor Leste) in the last decade? I couldn't imagine not having any books to read!

Love Kate x

Date: 21 September 

Hi Jamie

It has been fun to laze on the Thai beaches and swim in the clear waters. We stayed in Chang Mai the first week, looking after the elephants in the Elephant Nature Park. It was amazing – we got to feed and bathe them.

Kate x

Date: 29 September 

Hi Jamie

We are now in Vientiane, the capital of Laos. We hired some bicycles and rode to That Luang, a *stupa* (a hemisphere-shaped Buddhist building) covered in gold leaf. It glowed in the sunlight! We have tried some of the local foods. The best dish so far has been *laarp* (minced meat with ground rice and herbs). Delicious!

Say hi to everyone
Kate x

Date: 30 September 

Hi Kate

Your holiday sounds amazing! I've decided to research the places you visit on the Internet, so that I can picture what you are doing. Nothing much else has changed here at school … but the new skate park next door is finally open.

Stay in touch!
Jamie :)

Date: 4 October 

Hi Jamie

You must visit China! Beijing is incredible! I loved visiting the Forbidden City and climbing the Great Wall of China. Wish I'd had my skateboard today … Riding in a tuk tuk was frightening! It was definitely worth the ride to see the view.

Today we visited the thousands of Terracotta Warriors guarding Emperor Qin Shi Huang's tomb in Xi'an. It was strange standing on the edge of the pit, looking at the lines of warriors that were more than 2000 years old.

Kate x

Date: 6 October 

Hi Kate

I can't believe the Terracotta Warriors are more than 2000 years old! The historical buildings and artefacts you have described are so different from what we have in Australia … Although, some of the cultural celebrations are quite similar!

Can't wait to see your photos.
Jamie :)

Date: 18 October 

Dear Jamie

Thanks for your email. We are now in India, but have just come from Bhutan where we visited some monasteries perched high in the mountains. There was even a Centre for Gross National Happiness research!

We have spent the past week travelling through India. I have loved tasting local delicacies, such as *Dal Moth* (a spicy lentil mix) and *Petha* (a sweet candy). The local women look great in their colourful, embroidered saris and jangling gold bangles. Tomorrow we will visit the famous Taj Mahal. Can't wait!

Kate x

Date: 23 October 

Dear Jamie

We're almost at the end of our trip, stopping off in Singapore. Did you know it is the only island sovereign city-state in the world? Tonight we are going to see the sound and light show at the Gardens by the Bay. There are super trees there that collect rainwater and generate solar power.

Have loved exploring parts of Asia, but am now looking forward to coming home and telling everyone about it. See you soon!

Love Kate x

Breakaway tasks

Remembering

1 Make an alphabetical list of the countries Kate visited on her holiday.

2 What did Kate do in Chang Mai?

Understanding

3 This text includes a series of emails. What other text types could Kate have used to present similar information?

4 Complete a PMI graphic organiser to identify the pros, cons and interesting facts about the use of tuk tuks for transportation. Include a labelled diagram of a tuk tuk.

Applying

5 Imagine you are Jamie. Write a response to Kate's final email.

6 Research facts about the Great Wall of China, including why it was built. Use the Question web graphic organiser to record your new facts.

Analysing

7 Use a Venn diagram to record similarities and differences between an Australian and Asian location described in the text.

8 Develop guidelines for creating a successful and interesting email/ postcard.

Evaluating

9 Rank five places mentioned in the text in order of those you would most like to visit.

Creating

10 Create a travel brochure or pamphlet featuring one of the places Kate visited on her vacation. Include places to visit, interesting facts and fun activities to do.

Ambassador's speech

China and Australia's connections

"Engagement with China is not new to Victoria. In 1979, Victoria entered its sister-state relationship with China's Jiangsu province. Only a year later, in 1980, Melbourne and Tianjin established the first sister-city relationship between the two countries.

Of course, the people-to-people and trade links go much further back, when Chinese came to Victoria to mine, trade and do business in the goldfields in the 1850s.

The 'new' Australia, which grew from colonial roots with the discovery of Victoria's gold, was closely connected to China from the very beginning.

According to the latest census, there are now 214 000 Victorians with Chinese ancestry and 94 000 people born in China who have migrated here …

The dimensions and success of Australia's relationship with China are most easily described by trade figures and they are worth hearing.

It must have seemed unimaginable to our leaders when they established diplomatic relations with China back in 1972 – that two-way trade, then just $100 million a year, would four decades later exceed $120 billion …

Victoria welcomes more Chinese visitors than Canada (248 900) and New Zealand (145 500) do.

The number of Chinese visitors to Victoria who travel to Sovereign Hill (20%) and to Phillip Island (20%) demonstrates the importance of Victoria's historical connections to China and the appeal of its clean environment and diverse wildlife …

I look forward to seeing what the future will bring, and I know that if Australia, Victoria and China are involved, it will be exciting and well worth the wait."

Her Excellency Ms Frances Adamson, Australian Ambassador to China
Extract from Speech at the ACBC/Asialink luncheon:
Victoria and China at 40. Friday, 9 November 2012

Breakaway tasks

Remembering

1 Which Chinese city is Melbourne's sister city?

2 According to the latest census, how many Victorians are there with Chinese ancestry?

Understanding

3 Explain some of the reasons Chinese people like to visit Australia.

4 Describe how the Chinese were first connected with Victoria. What made Chinese people journey to Australia in the 1850s?

Applying

5 Predict what might happen in the future as more business trade occurs between Australia and China (consider trade, travel, shared customs, sport, food and hobbies). Draw a world map highlighting Australia and China. Draw links between the two countries and write some of your predictions near the linking lines.

6 Make a list of five jobs that the Australian ambassador would do to help promote Chinese–Australian relationships.

Analysing

7 What is the purpose of this speech?

8 Find out about the numbers of tourists coming to Australia from different Asian countries. Present your information in a graph.

Evaluating

9 Research the concept of sister cities. In your opinion, what is the strongest argument for having sister cities?

Creating

10 Create a commemorative plaque for an Australian city to present to a Chinese sister city. Think about the symbols you would include on the plaque.

Strands in action

Core tasks

1 Create an eMagazine showing comparisons between Asia and Australia.
   a Write a fact file about Australia and Asia/an Asian country, including information about the population, main languages, land area and religions.
   b Create a table that displays information about cultural traditions. Include the name of each country, the tradition and a description.
   c Create a visual display about food, fashion and hobbies.
   d Collate and present your information digitally.

2 Create a passport for yourself. As each student prepares and shares information about a chosen Asian country, collect stamps and stickers to fill your passport.
   a Design a passport for yourself.
   b Choose an Asian country to explore. Identify current interesting facts about your chosen country.
   c Present your findings to your classmates in an interesting way. Pinpoint your country on a world map and include a quiz.
   d Design a stamp or sticker that can be placed in your classmates' passports.
   e Invite families or community members to share information about these countries.

Extra tasks

1 Write a Haiku poem about an Asian tourist destination.

2 Create a fact file about a famous Asian invention that has changed the way Australians live.

3 Identify a traditional Asian game and learn how to play it.

4 List four reasons why it is important for Australia to have a strong relationship with Asian countries.

When reading, always remember to look at any visual information given, such as maps, tables, graphs, diagrams and photographs. These often provide you with extra valuable information on the topic you are reading about.